Bygone
BOURNEMOUTH

Alum Chine and St Ambrose's church.

Bygone
BOURNEMOUTH

Mary Davenport

Phillimore

1988

Published by
PHILLIMORE & CO. LTD.
Shopwyke Hall, Chichester, Sussex

ISBN 0 85033 676 7

Printed and bound in Great Britain by
BIDDLES LTD.
Guildford, Surrey

List of Illustrations

Frontispiece: Alum Chine and St Ambrose's church

Acknowledgements

I wish to express my thanks to the many people who have so kindly helped me in compiling this book, and for the loan of postcards and photographs. In particular I wish to thank Mr. Frank H. Beale, M.A., for his generous help throughout, for giving me so many details of old Bournemouth and for kindly reading the manuscript. I also wish to thank Mrs. Pamela Benton, Mr. Ian Taylor Brett, the *Royal Bath Hotel*, the De Vere Hotels; Bournemouth Museums; J. Arthur Dixon, Isle of Wight; Mr. David Dorey; Dorset County Library; Miss Carol Haynes, Mr. Philip Jones, the *Royal Exeter Hotel*, Berni Hotels Ltd., Mrs. Pamela Hamilton Howard; Hampshire County Cricket Club; Lens, Sutton; Mr. K.R.J. MacAlister, Bournemouth A.F.C.; Mr. Christopher T. Smith, *Highcliff Hotel*; Mr. and Mrs. Harold Roberts; and my husband for his tremendous assistance and enthusiasm.

Books by the same author

Newton Abbot in Old Picture Postcards
Plymouth in Old Picture Postcards
Poole in Old Picture Postcards

Plays
Alice in Wonderland
Through the Looking Glass
The Magic Bird

A place of infinite variety,
  Of music and of flowers,
Pines murmuring beside the sea.
  A happy haunt to spend the leisure hours
And dream the days away into Eternity.

This is not a history of Bournemouth nor a guide book, but rather a glimpse of bygone days, of how people and places looked in Victorian and Edwardian times, and on up to 1930. There have been great developments since Lewis Tregonwell bought land in 1810 above the little Bourne stream and built the first house there, occupying it in 1812. He was a man with vision, as were the many men who came after him and helped to develop Bournemouth.

The town has no ancient history as do its neighbours, Poole and Christchurch, whose roots go back hundreds of years. It is a curious fact that this glorious piece of coastline remained wild and lonely heathland for so many centuries. The first known reference to the stream 'La Bournemowthe' appears in the Christchurch Cartulary of 1407. The chines would have been boggy areas traversed only by a few fishermen who lived at inland villages, and in the 18th and 19th centuries by the smugglers whose ponies brought the tobacco, silks and wines landed from France on the seashore at dead of night. They would hide their contraband in the dense brushwood and thickets until the coast was clear to make their journeys overland. It was not unusual for horseback riders to lose their way travelling from Christchurch to Poole, so ill defined were the tracks. Frequently they would have to cross the moorland to the cliff edge to establish their direction. One notorious smuggler was Old Gulliver who is said to have employed up to fifty men wearing 'a kind of livery, powdered hair and frock coats'. This dress would no doubt have been donned when the waggons and horses had left Branksome Chine and were proceeding through the New Forest en route to London and large towns in the Midlands.

Mr. Tregonwell's house, which he called The Mansion, encouraged other owners of land to build fine houses. Sir George Tapps-Gervis was such a one and, with the inspired planting of thousands of pine trees in wide avenues, the resort was born. At first Bournemouth was considered primarily as a health resort, highly recommended by doctors as a suitable place for invalids. In 1841 Dr. A. B. Granville, author of *The Spas of England*, was invited to Bournemouth to give his opinion on the resort. At a public dinner given in his honour he said, 'Having examined Bournemouth in all its parts, under sunshine as well as during the prevalence of wet and high wind ... I have no hesitation in stating that no situation that I have had occasion to examine along the whole Southern coast possesses so many capabilities of being made the very first watering place in England; and not only a watering place but, what is still more important, a winter residence for the delicate constitutions requiring a warm and sheltered locality. It might be converted into a perfect blessing for those who do not like to tear themselves from home to go in search of foreign and salubrious climates.' This glowing tribute from the good doctor spread the length and breadth of the land and invalids flocked to Bournemouth.

Gradually this image changed as it was realised, towards the end of the First World War, that healthy visitors should be encouraged to visit the lovely resort as well as invalids. At this time the name of the charming Invalids' Walk was changed to the Pine Walk and the advantages of a family resort were advertised, with the motto *Pulchritudo et Salubritas*, 'Beauty and Health', incorporated into the Bournemouth crest. The town was frequented by members of royalty, including King Oscar of Sweden and Norway and his Queen Sophia Wilhelmina with their son Prince Oscar. The beautiful Elizabeth, Empress of Austria, loved Bournemouth and stayed at the *Royal Exeter Hotel*. Another royal visitor was our own Edward, Prince of Wales, later King Edward VII. He came first as a very young man with his tutor. Some years later he built a house in Derby Road. Kaiser Wilhelm II was a visitor whilst staying at Highcliffe Castle. He moored his yacht in the bay and his orchestra came ashore on 28 and 29 November 1907, giving two concerts at the Winter Gardens. Building took place everywhere as many more people came to retire and to spend their holidays in the new resort.

Change is not always welcomed, however. There was much opposition to the advent of the railway age, led by a local clergyman. A public meeting was held at which he recited:

'Tis well from far to hear the railway scream,
And watch the curling, lingering clouds of steam;
But let not Bournemouth health's approved abode,
Court the near presence of the iron road.

In spite of the clergyman's eloquence the vote went against him, the railway came and progress continued in the town. Victory had been won by the more far-sighted residents and councillors. William Gladstone, the 'Grand Old Man' of British politics, made his last public speech at Bournemouth railway station in 1898, concluding 'God bless you all, and this place, and the land we love'.

Many famous writers and artists have associations with Bournemouth. Robert Louis Stevenson came for his health in August 1884 and whilst staying at 'Skerryvore' in Alum Chine Road he wrote *Dr. Jekyll and Mr. Hyde* and also *Kidnapped*. A charming memorial garden has been laid out by the Bournemouth Corporation on the site of his former home . The son of the great poet Percy Bysshe Shelley, Sir Percy Florence Shelley, bought and developed the estate at Boscombe, calling the house Boscombe Manor. A great deal of memorabilia has been gathered there, relating to Shelley the poet and his family. The poet's heart lies with his son in the family tomb in St Peter's churchyard. Rupert Brooke spent much time in Bournemouth from his boyhood, since his grandfather, the Rev. Richard Brooke, retired to the town in 1895. The artist Aubrey Beardsley came to Bournemouth hoping to be cured of his illness. He stayed at 'Pier View', Boscombe, in 1896, and later at 'Muriel' in Exeter Road.

The town's high reputation for good music, established by Sir Dan Godfrey, the Director of the Bournemouth Municipal Orchestra in the 1890s, has spread throughout the British Isles and all over the world. Today, the famous Bournemouth Symphony Orchestra performs at its traditional home, the Winter Gardens, and visiting military bands give open-air concerts from the bandstand in the Lower Gardens throughout the summer season. The Theatre Royal in Albert Road was built in 1882. It cost £10,000 and could seat 1,000 people. Even in those days a number of London companies performed there, bringing with them many of the most famous actors and actresses of the day. In later years the establishment was refurbished and renamed the Bournemouth Theatre and Opera House. Fred Terry, Matheson Lang, Irene and Violet Vanbrugh all appeared at the theatre, and Julia Neilson performed in 'Sweet Nell of Old Drury'. Musicals were also put on by the Carl Rosa Opera Company.

Guglielmo Marconi, the great inventor to whom the modern world owes so much, knew Bournemouth well. He made his headquarters at the *Haven Hotel* in Sandbanks where he established one of his transmitting stations. He worked ceaselessly in his attempt to send messages across the Atlantic and was awarded the Nobel Peace Prize in 1909 for his valuable work in physics. Marconi was a great friend of Florence and Charles van Raalte who owned Brownsea Castle, where they entertained lavishly. It was here that Marconi met his future wife. His yacht *Elettra* was often moored off Brownsea Island and was used extensively for transmission.

It is fortunate that the rise of Bournemouth in the 19th century coincided with rapid advances in the art of photography. The output of picture postcards was prodigious and the halfpenny postage rate allowed the pastime of sending and collecting postcards to develop. Many of these pictures were minor works of art and make intriguing comparisons with modern scenes. Bournemouth's relatively late development has also meant that there is a lot of documentary evidence relating to the buildings and shops in the town, and the people who lived there in the early days.

The year 1910 was the centenary of the foundation of Bournemouth. There were many celebrations, including an exhibition of flying by distinguished aviators including the Hon. Charles Stewart Rolls, the first man to fly to France and back in a day. Tragically, the brave display was ended by an accident, and Charles Rolls was killed.

The area round Bournemouth is Thomas Hardy country, ancient Wessex. Hardy created the lovely name Sandbourne for this garden city by the sea. In *Tess of the d'Urbervilles* Angel Clare came to Sandbourne, or Bournemouth, in search of Tess:

> this fashionable watering-place with its eastern and western stations, its piers, its groves of pines, its promenades and its covered gardens, was to Angel Clare like a fairy palace, suddenly created by the stroke of the wand. An outlying eastern trace of the enormous Egdon waste was close at hand, yet on the very verge of that tawny antiquity such a glittering novelty as this pleasure city had chosen to spring up ... it was a city of detached mansions; a Mediterranean lounging place on the English Channel.

For

Suzibel and Gilles

1. A postcard of Bournemouth from the past. This interesting scene shows the leisurely pace of traffic in the town, the pedestrians casually crossing the roads, horse traffic and a veteran motor car in the Square. Many of the buildings shown here have now been demolished.

2. The Square, looking west, postmarked 1906. The name 'Square' evolved because of the shape of the important road junction at this point. The road from Poole led here, and then followed two possible routes to Christchurch, via either Old Christchurch Road or what is now Bath Road. There was a further road from Wimborne and the north down what is now Richmond Hill. In the early years many visitors would write to the local newspaper saying what a lot of time they had wasted trying to find an elusive address in the Square and even today this area of Bournemouth can be very confusing.

3. A closer view of the Square, showing the *Empress Hotel* with shops below. There are horse-drawn carriages plying for hire and the open-top tram bears the destination plate County Gates.

4.   Bournemouth pier approach in 1899.

5.   Bournemouth pier, *c*.1890.

6.   A charming view of the pier, a popular place to take the air and meet one's friends. Work on this pier was begun in 1878 and completed within two years. There was a day of celebration when the new pier was opened on 11 August 1880 by Sir Francis Wyatt Truscott, the Lord Mayor of London. It was said that at this time 'one might pace up and down and enjoy the beauties of sunrise and sunset, with the restless sea moving and surging around. The visitors are most of them too delicate to venture thereon, except when the mid-day sun has dispersed all chilliness from the atmosphere'.

7. On the pier: a card postmarked 1906. The sender writes, 'just come on the pier for a few hours with me, it's really lovely'. The clock at the entrance was presented by Mr. Horace Davey (later Lord Davey) who was the Member of Parliament for Christchurch, and represented Bournemouth.

8. A study of the pier and Undercliff Drive taken from the West Cliff walk. This is a romantic scene so it is small wonder that Bournemouth is especially popular for honeymoons.

9. The Pines, West Cliff, postmarked 1903. The peaceful setting and the ankle-length dresses of the ladies are of particular interest. The reverse of the postcard reads 'We are having a grand time, the weather is A1. B. is looking lovely, everywhere full of people. We went on the water to see the fleet last night. It was simply grand, never seen anything like it'.

10. Another view of the Pine Walk. These fine trees are a feature of the landscape of Bournemouth. They were planted extensively during the 19th century on land that was at the time a heather- and bracken-clad wilderness, stretching from Christchurch to Poole.

11. The scene from the West Cliff sent by the author's grandmother in 1904. The costumes of the children are especially interesting. Note the wide open space in front of the pier entrance, and the total lack of traffic!

12.   The West Cliff shelters, the lift and the pier. This was a very popular place for a walk, then as now. In spite of their ankle-length hobble skirts and large, wide-brimmed hats, many ladies carried parasols to keep off the sun.

13.   On the West Cliff four elegant mansions were built in 1873-4, known as the Highcliffe Mansions. They had magnificent views overlooking the sea and, to the east, the town of Bournemouth. A short time later they were joined together to become the *Highcliffe Hotel*. This opened just before Christmas 1874, to cater for the 'carriage trade', for the town was fast becoming a fashionable place in which to spend a holiday. It is interesting to note that Highcliffe is spelt with an 'e'. This has now disappeared. Further east was the resort of Highcliffe with its hotel of that name. Much confusion arose and so the hotel owners decided who should retain the 'e' by the toss of a coin. The Bournemouth hotel lost the toss, and so it is known today as the *Highcliff*.

14.   In the beautifully manicured gardens of the *Highcliff Hotel* stand these old coastguard cottages, built in the early 19th century. It was a lonely spot in those days for the men whose duty it was to guard the coastline and to watch out for smugglers, including the most notorious, 'Old Gulliver'. He found the deserted chines ideal places for making a quick getaway after landing tobacco, brandy, lace and silks from France. Today these cottages have been renovated inside to provide luxurious suites for hotel guests, whilst retaining their exterior rustic charm.

15.   'Smugglers at Bourne Mouth', painted by Henry Perlee Parker (1795-1873). The central figure is believed to be Old Gulliver.

16. St Michael's Road, West Cliff, much of which remains today and should survive as the road has been made a conservation area. It is interesting for the varied styles of architecture displayed.

17. At the beginning of the 19th century the county border was at Durley Chine. By 1818 it had been moved to Alum Chine, and here it remained throughout Victorian and Edwardian days, and up to 1974 when Bournemouth became part of the county of Dorset.

18. County Gates, once the demarcation line between Dorset and Hampshire.

PIER AND SANDS FROM DURLEY CHINE, BOURNEMOUTH   116

19.   The cliffs and foreshore at Durley Chine, a popular beach with holiday-makers. The name Durley is thought to come from Durley near Bishop's Waltham. The name appears on a local map of 1805 when the land with the chine became the property of William Dean.

20.   This remarkable sand sculpture was made on the beach at Bournemouth in 1935 by J. Suchomlin. Using only sand, water and colour, it represents the flight into Egypt of Mary and Joseph, with the baby Jesus. Such artistry is rarely seen on any beaches today.

THE FLIGHT INTO EGYPT.

MODELLED IN SAND BY J. SUCHOMLIN.
BOURNEMOUTH 1935.
ONLY SAND, WATER AND COLOUR USED.

21.   The rustic bridge in Alum Chine. Running inland from the sea for nearly a mile, the boggy land of former days has now been drained to make a beautiful shady walk. It was here in 1892 that the young Winston Churchill, whilst playing with his younger brother and cousin, leapt from a bridge into a fir tree and fell to the ground 29 feet below. He was at that time staying with his aunt and uncle, Lord and Lady Wimborne, at 'Branksome Dene'.

22.   This view from the Alum Chine Suspension Bridge will be familiar to many older residents, although it is much changed today. Just above the entrance to Alum Chine stood 'Skerryvore', once home of Robert Louis Stevenson and now a memorial garden for him.

23. Skerryvore, the Bournemouth home of Robert Louis Stevenson from 1885 to 1887.

24. Cliff Cottage, West Cliff, in 1863. Charles Darwin stayed at the cottage in 1862. Until 1981 it was the site of the *Regent Palace Hotel*.

25. The lush foliage of the walk through Alum Chine. Mining was started here in the 16th century by James Blount, sixth Baron Mountjoy and Lord of the Manor of Canford, who discovered alum on his estate and hoped to produce enough to supply the English market. Large quantities were used in the tanning trade and at that time it was imported from Italy. However, the venture was not a success, investors lost their money and the Baron was ruined, dying in poverty in 1581. The church in the background is St Ambrose's, the parish church of Westbourne.

26.   This scene will be familiar to many for it is here that Alum Chine meets the sea. The sands are fine and yellow, the plants luxuriant in growth, palms and yuccas abound. The Purbeck hills provide a perfect backdrop.

27.   Joseph's Steps on the West Cliff, leading to Durley Chine. These were built by Joseph Cutler, using timber from the wrecked pier of 1861. The pier had many mishaps from the beginning. Its building was delayed because of disagreements regarding its construction, it suffered in the early stages from rough seas and then the bank which held the Commissioners' funds failed. However, money was loaned by the National Provincial Bank at Poole and work proceeded. After the pier was finally opened by Sir George Gervis in September 1861, it was attacked by the marine pest the teredo, and the piles were so weakened that they could not withstand the winter storms. By 1877 it was damaged beyond repair.

28.   The charming residence Branksome Tower, built in 1855 by Mr. C. W. Packe for his own use on the Branksome Tower Estate. Fine trees surrounded the house. At the entrance to the private road (now the Avenue) was a Lodge and an iron gate and stone pillars, known as County Gates. In later years the house was sold and became the *Branksome Tower Hotel*, considered one of the finest on this coast.

29.   A view of the verandah leading to the lounge of the *Branksome Tower Hotel*, *c*.1920. The beautiful gardens with masses of hydrangeas and roses were a feature much enjoyed by the many visitors. The building has been demolished and is now a block of flats.

30.   A rare postcard of the Herbert Home, built as a memorial to Lord Sidney Herbert of Lea (1810-61), the Member of Parliament for Wiltshire from 1832. As Secretary of War 1852-55 he was much concerned to improve sanitation and health conditions within the Army. It was through him that his close friend Florence Nightingale, who lived at Embley Park near Romsey, went out to Scutari during the Crimean War to nurse the wounded. Lord Herbert died at Wilton House and his many friends decided that a suitable memorial would be a convalescent home for the poor and the weak. This splendid building in Alumhurst Road was the result.

31.   On the West Cliff, looking towards Swanage. The sandy path, pines and rhododendrons, with gorse and wild flowers, give an impression of the peace and solitude to be found here.

32.   This view of the West Cliff is of particular interest for the costumes of the walkers, and for the sandy paths winding between the pines.

33.   Middle Chine descends from the West Cliff Drive to the sea. Over the years Bournemouth Council has done some remarkable work in maintaining the Drive.

Upper Gardens, Bournemouth.

34. Postmarked 1914, this card shows the wild scrub and gorse in Middle Chine. In Victorian days the tracks through the chine were overgrown and boggy, in many cases known only to a few fishermen and the smugglers with their pack horses picking their way through the dense undergrowth.

35. The Upper Gardens with the Congregational church. Well-wooded with carefully tended lawns and flower beds, these gardens provided a quiet and level walk surprisingly near the busy town.

36. The view from Mont Dore, looking across the gardens to the sea. This postcard was sent by the author's grandmother in 1907.

37. The Gardens and Mont Dore. This fine building was originally the *Mont Dore Hotel*, so called by Dr. Horace Dobell who had come to live in Bournemouth and decided to establish a spa, having been impressed by the Mont Dore Cure given in the Auvergne, France. The hotel opened in the summer of 1885 and was said to be the finest building in the town. Besides being a hotel, it was a hydropathic spa with mineral and vapour baths, waters for the cure being imported from the Auvergne. The interior was luxurious, with ornately decorated drawing-rooms, billiard and smoking rooms, and even a covered tennis court.

38. The beautifully situated war memorial with the town hall, established here in 1921 in the former *Mont Dore Hotel*. It stood in four acres of grounds in an area known as the Glen and was Italianate in style. In the basement of the hotel, seawater baths were available and, for Turkish baths, fresh water was pumped from the Bourne stream. During World War One the building became a military hospital.

39. An early view of The Mansion, the first house to be built in Bournemouth. In 1810 whilst the Tregonwells were on holiday at Mudeford, they journeyed over the heath along the coast. Mr. Tregonwell knew the coast well as he had commanded the Dorset Rangers. His wife was charmed with the delightful spot where the Bourne stream ran down to the sea and said she would like to have a holiday home there. The owner of the land was Sir George Ivison Tapps, Lord of the Manor of Christchurch. Tregonwell purchased 8½ acres of land for £179 10s. The Mansion was completed in 1812.

40. Lewis Tregonwell (1758-1832), the founder of Bournemouth.

41. The *Tregonwell Arms* in 1883. Originally the *Tapps Arms*, it was a favourite meeting place for smugglers. The *Tregonwell*, demolished in 1884, had tea gardens which were very popular with summer visitors because of the beautiful views of the bay.

Built by Squire Tregonwell about 1810.
Called Tregonwell House.
Name Altered to Portman Lodge
When it was occupied
by Lord Portman.

The Second House built in Bournemouth 1700

42.   This charming thatched building was the second house built in Bournemouth by Lewis
Tregonwell, for his butler, Symes, and called Tregonwell House. After she was widowed in
1832, Mrs. Henrietta Tregonwell lived here until 1846. She changed the name to Portman
Lodge after her father's family, the Portmans of Orchard Portman and Bryanston, near
Blandford in Dorset.

43. *Newlyn's Royal and Imperial Hotel*, known today as the *Royal Exeter Hotel*. The building was called Exeter House when it was purchased in 1870 by Mr. Henry Newlyn for use as a hotel. Before this time it had been the home of the Marchioness of Exeter from whom the present name derives. In later years the house became a private school for boys.

44. A view of *Newlyn's Hotel* from another angle. So successful was the hotel that a new wing was added in 1876 and it was enlarged again in 1886. The original house was retained intact, so the present structure contains part of the first house ever built in Bournemouth. *Newlyn's Hotel* had many distinguished visitors, including Her Imperial Majesty, the Empress Elizabeth of Austria, with her daughter, the Archduchess Marie Valerie. They arrived with their entourage on 10 April 1888, staying about ten days, taking over the entire hotel for the visit. The Empress brought 30 servants and seven tons of luggage.

45.   A portrait of Mr. Henry Newlyn, the owner of *Newlyn's Royal and Imperial Hotel*. He associated himself
with many events and projects for the improvement of Bournemouth. He became an alderman and was Mayor
of Bournemouth in 1892 and again in 1895. He was also a Justice of the Peace. Before the incorporation of
the Borough, Henry Newlyn had been Chairman of the Board of Commissioners.

46. A portrait of Mrs. Leonie Newlyn, who assisted her husband Henry in the management of their hotel. She played an active part in the life of Bournemouth during her time as mayoress. The beautiful Victorian dress and shawl, with the charming mob cap, are reminiscent of the period.

47.   A corner of Mr. and Mrs. Henry Newlyn's private suite.

48. The Billiard Room of the *Royal Exeter Hotel*.

49. The comfortable Residents' Lounge in the *Royal Exeter Hotel*, during the days of Mr. Henry Newlyn.

50. An interesting menu from *Newlyn's Hotel*, dated 15 October 1896. Many of the courses are familiar today. The Pudding à la Nesselrode was a Victorian iced pudding, flavoured with chestnuts and Maraschino, created by Mony, chef to the famous Count Nesselrode. The average cost was 3s. 6d.

Menu.

WINE—
Chablis.

Amontillado.

Marcobrunner.

Wachtér's
Royal Charter
Champagne.

Château La Rose.

LIQUEURS—
Port, 1863.

NEWLYN'S HOTEL,
Oct. 15th, 1896.

Native Oysters.
—:—
Clear Turtle.
Palestine.
—:—
Crimped Codfish.   Oyster Sce.
Soles à la Colbert.
—:—
Boudins de Volaille à la Reine.
Mutton Cutlets à la reforme.
—:—
Haunch of Venison,
French Beans.   Mashed Potatoes.
—:—
Pheasants.
Artichokes à la crème.
Potato Chips.
—:—
Apricot Tarts.   Apple Charlotte.
Noyeau Jellies.   Jubilee Creams.
Eclairs au Chocolât.   Meringues.
—:—
Pudding à la Nesselrode.
Stilton.   Cheddar.   Gorgonzola
Coffee.
—:—
Dessert.

51. The *Royal Exeter Hotel*. Whilst staying here in 1886, the Empress of Austria had no interpreter and, although the Empress herself spoke some English, it was difficult for her staff to make themselves understood. A cow was kept in the Priory stables opposite the hotel and milk was taken for Her Majesty, under the supervision of her own doctor. She was also very fond of hot sea-water baths, and the water for these was supplied from the sea-water baths of Messrs. Roberts & Co., situated near the pier. Her attendants had difficulty in explaining whether milk or water was required, so the gardener was labelled with miniature sandwich boards; the one on his back said 'cow' and the one on his chest said 'sea-water'. He wore these during the day and when water was required he was poked in the chest, and if milk was needed he was slapped on the back.

52. A scene on the West Cliff, where the Empress of Austria would have strolled in the early mornings with Mrs. Leonie Newlyn. She hoped to return the following year, but was assassinated on the lakeside in Geneva whilst about to board a lake steamer. The assassin had vowed to kill the first royal person he encountered.

53.   A peaceful scene at Children's Corner, the little Bourne stream carrying the sailing boats placidly along.

54.   A later view of Children's Corner, showing what was then known as the 'New Bandstand'.

CHILDREN'S CORNER
AND NEW BANDSTAND,
BOURNEMOUTH.

55.   This view is of particular interest for the costumes of the four people in the foreground. The gardens were beautifully wooded at that time – the card is postmarked 1905.

56.   This delightful old postcard shows the East Cliff and paths before the advent of the Undercliff Drive. The bathing machines drawn up against the cliff were pulled down to the water's edge so that ladies could modestly enter the sea, without being seen walking down the sands in their bathing costumes, though these often covered them from neck to toe.

57. The Undercliff Drive, pier and East Cliff walk. A pleasure steamer is alongside the pier. Steamship services were a great attraction during the summer months, making daily calls. The most popular steamer in the early days was *Heather Bell*, owned by George Burt of Swanage. There were regular sailings to Poole and Swanage, and weekly excursions to the Isle of Wight and Lulworth.

58. The S.S. *Prince of Wales*, frequently seen off the coast of Bournemouth at the turn of the century. She was one of a fleet of pleasure steamers which included the *Balmoral, Lorna Doone, Queen, Solent Queen* and others. They sailed from Southampton, Southsea, the Isle of Wight, Bournemouth, Swanage, Weymouth, and across to Cherbourg.

59. The S.S. *Brodick Castle* sailed daily from April to October, to the Isle of Wight, Brighton, Weymouth and Southampton. For many years her master was Captain Tilsed, a well-known character on this coast.

60. The *Bath Hotel*, designed by Benjamin Ferrey of Christchurch, as it looked in Victorian times. The hotel was opened with great ceremony on Queen Victoria's Coronation Day, 28 June 1838, by Sir George Gervis. The hotel was completed only a few weeks before the opening. The rough tree-lined road gives a good idea of the area at that time. Commanding striking views to the sea and across the bay, the hotel quickly attracted the cream of Victorian society. Amongst the distinguished visitors were His Royal Highness Edward Prince of Wales, Benjamin Disraeli, W. E. Gladstone, the Empress Eugenie of Sweden and the King of the Belgians. The nearest railway stations were at Poole and Christchurch, so shortly after the hotel opened a horse coach service was started to transport the many visitors.

61. The frontage of the *Royal Bath Hotel* after it was bought in 1876 by Merton Russell-Cotes, a wealthy traveller and art collector who had visited Bournemouth for his health. Learning that the owner of the *Bath Hotel*, Mr. A. Briant, wished to sell, Russell-Cotes saw this fine building as a suitable place to display his many antiques and rare paintings, as well as retaining it as a hotel. Two new wings were added to the existing structure, although this was considered very rash by some local residents. It became the *Royal Bath Hotel* and as such was re-opened by Sir Francis Wyatt Truscott, the Lord Mayor of London, on 11 August 1880.

Royal Visitors to Bournemouth Hotels

During the last 20 years ending February 1st, 1890.

ROYAL BATH AND EAST CLIFF HOTEL.

ESTABLISHED 1838.

Year	Names of Visitors.	Length of Stay.
1881.	Ex-Empress Eugenie	2 hours.
1887.	H.R.H. Duchess of Albany H.R.H. Crown Princess of Denmark	} 26 hours.

ROYAL AND IMPERIAL
EXETER PARK HOTEL.

ESTABLISHED 1870

1872.	Princess Brezenheim Princess Windischgratz	} 3 weeks.
1881.	Prince Soltykoff Princess Soltykoff Prince Jean Soltykoff Princess Elizabeth Soltykoff Princess Seraphine Soltykoff Princess Anna Soltykoff	} 10 days.
1888.	**Her Imperial Majesty The Empress- Queen of Austro-Hungary** **Her Imperial and Royal Highness The Archduchess Marie Valerie**	} 7 days.

And a Suite of twenty-eight Persons.

The whole of the Hotel was reserved by Royal Command
for TEN days.

Prince and Princess Bernadotte called on H.I. Majesty.

62. Bournemouth was very proud of its many distinguished visitors as this pamphlet, issued on 1 February 1890, clearly shows. It lists not only the names of the royal visitors but how long they stayed at the *Royal Bath* and *East Cliff Hotel* and the *Royal and Imperial Exeter Park Hotel*, during the 20 years from 1870 to 1890.

63. This delightful walk from Westover Gardens to the *Royal Bath Hotel* was a great favourite with visitors to the town, especially the invalids who came from every corner of the country, seeking renewed health amongst the pines and beside the sea. Of especial interest is the Bournemouth coat-of-arms, bearing the motto *Pulchritudo Et Salubritas*, Beauty and Health.

64. The morbid name Invalids' Walk was replaced by the appropriate Pine Walk by the end of World War One.

65. The splendid glass structure named the Winter Gardens was completed in 1877. After the success of the 1851 Crystal Palace Exhibition in London it became fashionable for seaside resorts to follow suit. Built on land formerly part of the Tregonwell estate, this building was a great addition to the cultural life of Bournemouth. There was seating accommodation for 800, in amongst palms and exotic shrubs. The Winter Gardens cost £12,000, and was opened by the M.P. for Christchurch, Sir H. Drummond Wolff, on 16 January 1877.

66. Another view of the Winter Gardens, c.1898. It was not a success as an exhibition hall and became a concert hall in 1893 when the Council took over the lease, and the Bournemouth Municipal Orchestra was born, with Dan Godfrey Jnr. as Musical Director.

67.   The portrait of a remarkable man, John Elmes Beale, 1848-1928, founder of the renowned department store and Mayor of Bournemouth, 1902-1904. A man of vision, he played a great part in the shaping of Bournemouth as we know it today. He was the driving force behind the creation of the Undercliff Drive and the Pavilion. During his three years as mayor he was greatly assisted by Mrs. Beale, who has been described as 'able, amiable, gracious and courteous' in all the many things she did on behalf of the town.

68. The first premises of the firm of J. E. Beale, c. 1883. The name 'Fancy Fair' was adopted – with the opening of the railway, large numbers of visitors were anticipated, and for these Mr. Beale stocked wooden spades and tin buckets, children's boats, costing from one penny each, Japanese sunshades, walking sticks and string bags. Mr. and Mrs. Beale worked long hours in their shop. Wood from packing cases was used to make shelves and fittings, string, paper and cardboard were all saved to be used again. Glazed cardboard boxes were cut up for window and price tickets.

69. This splendid photograph of the annual outing of the staff of J. E. Beale was taken in 1895. Mr. Beale is standing on the right at the front, with Mrs. Beale seated next to him. Everyone looks rather solemn because they had to remain quite still for several seconds for the photographer to get the correct exposure. There was no instant snapping in those days.

ALDERMAN &
MRS J.E.BEALE
MAYOR &
MAYORESS
OF
BOURNEMOUTH
1902-3
1903-4
1904-5

70. A souvenir postcard of Alderman and Mrs. J. E. Beale, Mayor and Mayoress of Bournemouth. Mayor Beale was closely connected with the development of the Undercliff Drive. In 1903 a deputation was appointed to visit other seaside towns with similar cliff formation to Bournemouth, to see what could be learnt from them. The deputation consisted of the mayor, two aldermen, two councillors, the town clerk and the borough engineer. During September they toured the defensive works of resorts on the continent, visiting Ostend and Scheveningen, and also several east coast towns in England. Pavilions and Kursaals were noted, as they considered a 'central rendezvous' would be essential in Bournemouth's seafront development.

71. A view of the J. E. Beale building in the 1930s, in Art Deco style. Sadly this magnificent structure is no more, having been demolished by German bombs on 23 May 1943. It is still remembered with affection by many Bournemouth residents. The building has now been rebuilt to a pleasant post-war design.

72. An early J. E. Beale delivery van, *c.*1924, a familiar sight on the streets of Bournemouth.

73.   The opening of the Undercliff Drive was a great achievement, as the project had been debated for many years before being implemented. The most forward-looking councillors realised the drive was necessary to stop the erosion of the cliffs.

74.   Work on the Undercliff Drive had begun in January 1907. By November the first part was opened, running from the pier to Meyrick Road. The first section to the west was opened in June 1911. Mr. Russell-Cotes had been a great enthusiast for the building of the Undercliff Drive. To show his pleasure at the fruition of the scheme, he gave the town his remarkable collection of art treasures on the day it was opened. At the same time his wife, Annie Nelson Russell-Cotes, gave their home, East Cliff Hall (a birthday present to her from her husband), to create an Art Gallery and Museum for the benefit of the general public.

75. The Undercliff Drive, postmarked 1911, and especially interesting for the varied forms of transport portrayed.

76. A fairy-tale view of the Russell-Cotes Museum, as seen from the garden. The balustrade leads to the many rooms filled with the most delightful and unexpected treasures.

77. A corner of the Russell-Cotes Museum, showing some of the fine marble busts collected over many years. In recognition of their generous gift, Merton and Annie Russell-Cotes were made Honorary Freemen of the Borough. In 1909 a knighthood was bestowed on Merton Russell-Cotes for services to Bournemouth.

78. St Peter's church, from an engraving published *c*.1860.

79. St Peter's church, the elegant mother church of Bournemouth. There had earlier been a temporary building for Church of England services. This consisted of two semi-detached cottages. St Peter's church was built in 1843 and for two years it remained unconsecrated. The enthusiasm of the vicar, the Rev. Alexander Morden Bennett, and of G. E. Street, the architect, was responsible for the transformation of this original church; only the clock remained, with its face inside the tower. With the raising of the spire, the new church was completed and a thanksgiving service was held on 18 December 1879. Sadly, the Rev. Bennett died just one month later, on 19 January 1880.

80. Gervis Place with St Peter's church, *c.*1906, showing one of the early trams bound for the Square. The distinguished looking Arcade Chambers house the Stock Exchange Bureau and the offices of Jolliffe and Flint. The cupola is at the Gervis Place entrance to the Arcade.

81. The Rustic Bridge, from an 1855 engraving. This area is now covered by the site of the Gervis Arcade, popularly known as the Bournemouth Arcade. Money left by Sir George Gervis for the development of the town was used to build the bridge.

82. St Stephen's church was erected as a memorial to the Rev. Morden Bennett. It was designed by J. L. Pearson and begun in 1881. The first part was completed four years later, and on 10 June 1885 Dr. Harold Brown, Bishop of Winchester, consecrated the nave. It was here in 1888 that Prince Oscar, second son of King Oscar II of Norway and Sweden, was married to Miss Ebba Munck of Fulkila, according to the rites of the Swedish National Church.

83. The invitation sent by Her Majesty the Queen of Norway and Sweden to Mr. Henry Newlyn to attend the wedding of Prince Oscar to Miss Ebba Munck, on Thursday 15 March 1888 at 12.30 p.m. Later in the day the Prince renounced his claim to the Swedish throne and assumed the style of Prince Bernadotte. His son, Count Folke Bernadotte, was to become the United Nations Peace Envoy. He was assassinated in Palestine in 1948.

By Order of Her Majesty, The Queen of Sweden and Norway, the Chamberlain in Waiting has the honour to invite

Mr. H. Newlyn

to be present at St Stephen's Church, Bournemouth, on the occasion of the Wedding of Prince Oscar of Sweden and Norway, with Miss Ebba Munck, on Thursday, March 15th 1888, at 12.30 p.m.

84. The Scottish church and Richmond Hill in 1879.

85. The same area 50 years later, in 1929.

86. A view of the fine interior of the Congregational church with a portrait of the well-known and honoured pastor, the Rev. John Daniel Jones. 'J. D.', as he was known, came to Richmond Hill in 1898, and remained here until he retired in 1937. He was an eloquent preacher and became known throughout the English-speaking world. The author of many devotional books, he wrote his autobiography *Three score years and ten* in 1940. He died at Bala on 19 April 1942.

87. The Congregational church, Richmond Hill, was designed in 1889 and completed in 1891. The original church was not large enough for the growing number of worshippers nor was it thought to be sufficiently dignified. Thus the beautiful church we know today was built.

88.   Lansdowne is an important road junction and for many years a stone horse trough and drinking fountain were to be found here. The name is generally thought to have come from Somerset: Bath has the renowned Lansdowne Crescent. The name was first used in Bournemouth for the Lansdowne Villas, built on the north side of Christchurch Road. A few years later there was a *Lansdowne Hotel*, Lansdowne House and Lansdowne Crescent, and so the name became firmly associated with that part of the town.

89.   The coming of the railway influenced the development of the Westbourne district. The Arcade was built by Henry Joy, who was the builder of the Arcade in Bournemouth itself. He lived at Seamoor House, now demolished. The first shop in Westbourne Arcade was occupied in January 1885 and there were five shops by the end of the year.

90.   The East Cliff sands at the turn of the century, with a good view of the Fancy Bazaar and the refreshment hut on the sands. Large numbers of rowing boats can be seen plying for hire, and a long row of bathing machines at the sea edge in the distance. The cliffs were in constant danger of erosion by the high seas and winter storms.

91.   A jolly family party on the beach at Bournemouth, 1884. The costumes are of particular interest: the boaters and bonnets of the era and the frills and furbelows worn by the younger members of the family. This photograph was taken in front of Sydenham's Baths and Reading Rooms. A family outing such as this would require meticulous planning in Victorian days and would be a red-letter day, long remembered.

92. A postcard of the East Cliff sands, sent in 1906. Note the group of fishermen chatting in the foreground. At the Fancy Bazaar all manner of seaside requisites could be purchased.

93. Bournemouth pier on Regatta Day, August 1910. The steamers are the *Balmoral*, the *Bournemouth Queen* and the *Stirling Castle*; in the distance is the steamship *Duchess of Kent*.

The Belle Vue Hotel Library and Baths
BOURNEMOUTH 1855

94.   The *Belle Vue Hotel* was one of the earliest buildings in Bournemouth, situated at the foot of the gardens opposite the pier, and originally called the Belle Vue Boarding House. In 1842 it was said to be fitted up 'with every regard to elegance and comfort'. It contained a west wing with a library and reading-room, run by Mr. Sydenham. Later these were removed to the shop at the corner of Bath Road. This charming old drawing shows how it must have looked in 1855. It was demolished to provide a sea view for the new Pavilion, opened in March 1929.

95. The influence of Merton Russell-Cotes was largely responsible for the renewed interest in the building of a Pavilion. He had written to the local press in 1901 saying 'a seaside pavilion is an absolute necessity'. The deputation of 1903, headed by the Mayor, Alderman J. E. Beale, had done much research on pavilions, whilst working on the question of the Undercliff Drive. They reported: 'a pavilion, embracing a concert room, reading rooms, cafés (indoor and outdoor refreshments) and all other accommodation and advantages found in the very best of the kind we have seen on our travels should be provided in Bournemouth'.

96. The Pavilion and fountains by night. This attractive feature drew many visitors here on their evening strolls.

97.   The Municipal College is one of the finest buildings in the area. In 1913 the College and the Central Public Library were established at the Lansdowne. The College was designed by the Borough architect, F. W. Lacey, on the grounds of two freehold properties, 'Peachley' and 'Strathearn', purchased by the Corporation from Sir George Meyrick. The clock with its four faces was a gift to the town from Mrs. Croft, mother of local M.P. Henry Page Croft.

98.   The parish of Holy Trinity was created in November 1867. This Anglican church was erected in Madeira Vale in what was mainly a residential district. Five trustees, of whom John Tregonwell, the son of Lewis, was one, all guaranteed £3,000 to provide the endowment for a living.

99.   The Lymington-Poole mail coach, 1832. The coach road between Southampton and Poole was constructed in 1810 and ran through Bourne Bottom, near the site of the present Bournemouth town hall.

100.   An early view of the Square, bustling with horse-drawn carriages.

101.   West Station was opened on 15 June 1874 and was important to the future development of the town. In 1870 a branch line was extended from Christchurch to the edge of the Commissioners' District and became Bournemouth East Station. Prior to the opening of these two stations, the nearest rail links were at Holmsley station, Christchurch, from 1862, and Poole station, Hamworthy, from 1847. Travellers from either of these stations bound for Bournemouth had a further journey by horse omnibus or carriage. Mr. Russell-Cotes on enquiring at Waterloo for a ticket to Bournemouth was informed by the booking-clerk that he had never heard of the place.

102.   This small tank engine at Bournemouth Central was designed by Drummond. There were 105 of these engines built between 1897 and 1911, all very similar – the 'M7' class. They operated for many years, only being withdrawn after 1960. Several worked on the West of England lines.

103.   This engine pulling the express train from Bournemouth Central in 1905 was one of a series of about 60 engines built between 1899 and 1901 to the designs of Dugald Drummond, the Locomotive Superintendent of the London and South-Western Railway, 1895-1912. They were 4-4-0 express passenger engines, officially 'T9' class, and were very long lived, continuing in service on secondary duties until the days of British Rail, some surviving virtually until the end of steam in the 1960s.

104.   A rare photograph of the Bournemouth Aviation Meeting in July 1910, showing the Hon. C. S. Rolls in the air. Shortly after this photograph was taken he met with his tragic accident.

105.   Varied transport in the Square in 1909, including horse-drawn carriages and trams. There were no trams in Bournemouth before 1902.

106.   A few years later we see a taxi rank, open-topped trams crowded with passengers, and a two-horse brake with its driver dressed in white.

The Square, Bournemouth

107. Trolley buses were introduced on main routes in the mid-1930s. The tram shelter and boarding-point was being used by a motor bus when this photograph was taken.

108. A view of the Square looking towards the large department store of Bobby's, now Debenham's. The bus and coach station has since burnt down and the site is now a car park.

109. An idyllic cameo of the Lower Walk, postmarked 1907. By this time Bournemouth was attracting visitors for pleasure and for the beauty of its setting, as well as for health reasons. All could enjoy the pleasant walks, pure air, golden sands and the pine woods.

110. An unusual view of the *Royal Bath Hotel* and gardens, with the Isle of Wight in the distance. The statues have now been removed and there is a swimming pool in the grounds. This card is postmarked 1908.

THE ROYAL BATH
AND
EAST CLIFF HOTEL
BOURNEMOUTH
LOOKING TOWARDS ISLE OF WIGHT

111. An animated scene outside
Beale's store which was advertising
the arrival of Father Christmas by
aeroplane. The horse-drawn coach
carries the local band, and staff had
crowded to the upper windows,
peeping over the rocking horses to get
a good view of the crowd below. This
annual event became quite a carnival
procession through the town and
continued into the 1960s.

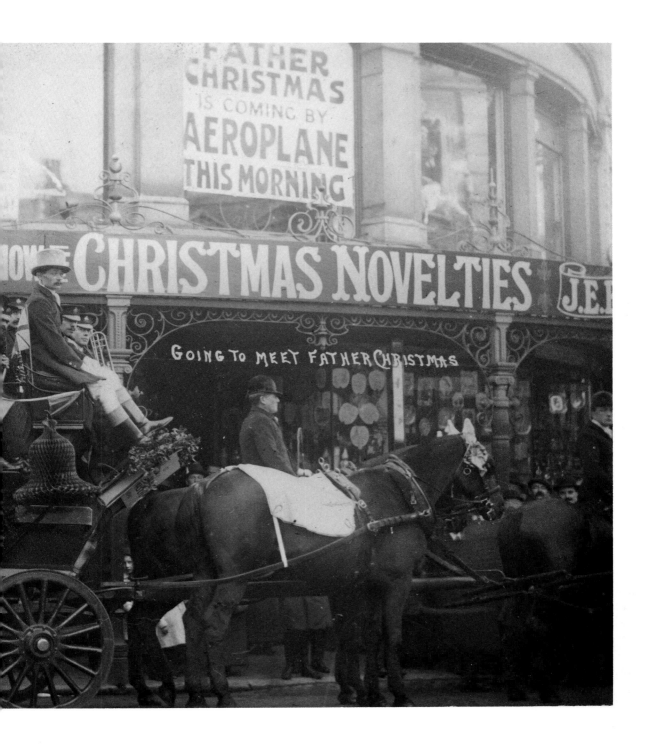

112.   There was tremendous excitement before Christmas 1912 when it was announced that Father Christmas would be arriving by aeroplane. With Cyril Beale dressed as Father Christmas, this primitive aeroplane flew over the store and landed in Meyrick Park. The traditional costume was made by Mrs. Beale. She did not think she would finish it in time, and had insufficient material for the hood; thus Beale's Father Christmas has never worn one.

113.   Meyrick Park as it appeared in Edwardian days. Early in the reign of George V aerobatic displays were frequently seen over the park. Gustav Hamel, the popular aviator, broke the record for 'looping the loop' on 11 April 1914.

114. Meyrick Park golf links. This 18-hole course was the first municipal golf course in the country. It was laid out under the supervision of Tom Dunn, the Bournemouth professional up to 1899.

115. The Drumhead Church Parade at Meyrick Park, June 1912. Five years earlier some boys from Bournemouth Boys Brigade took part in the very first Scout camp on Brownsea Island. Lord Baden-Powell had received permission from the van Raaltes to hold an experimental camp on the island for boys from widely different backgrounds. Twenty boys were chosen, from Eton, Harrow, the East End of London and the Bournemouth area. The camp was such a success that it became a model for boys' and girls' camp activities all over the world.

116. Children's Day in Meyrick Park, 21 June 1905, led by the Mayor's carriage drawn by a pair of fine horses. The Silver Band follows with a procession of children and townsfolk. Gaily decorated floats can be seen stretching away into the distance.

Meyrick Park June 21st 1905
Witkins photo

Bournemouth Centenary Grotesque Carnival.
"The Whale Car"

117.   In 1910 the Centenary Fêtes were held to celebrate the founding of Bournemouth. The town was decorated with flags and bunting, and the festivities lasted from 6 to 16 July. This picture shows one of the floats taking part in a procession, 'The Whale Car'. A splendid programme of sports and entertainments with elaborate carnival processions and confetti battles was organised.

118.   A corner of the East Cliff walk showing the thatched shelter, a haven when south-westerly winds were blowing.

119.   A pastoral view of Manor Road, with the row of donkey carriages drawn up to wait for invalids. These one-seat carriages were used to transport them down to the pier and the town. Looking rather like bath chairs, they must have been a very pleasant way in which to 'take the air'.

120.   There are few resorts in England with so many acres of continuous gardens leading off the main shopping centre. The beautiful Central Gardens seen here are a source of constant enjoyment for all who stroll in them. The names of the gardens have been changed from time to time but the well-tended lawns and the lovely flower beds, changing with the seasons, are always a joy to see.

121. An early view of the Square, showing the leisurely pace of life in that age.

122. The Square at the turn of the century, full of carriages. Note the ladder, which was used to mount the high brake. On the reverse of the card the sender writes, 'I quite forgot to mention in my letter the terms I think: 2 guineas, Cooking, Attendance and Light inclusive. Fire and hot baths extra. I did not come across any rooms in my wanderings less than this, many of them more. I do hope this is not too much'.

123.   The exquisite drawing of Lillie Langtry by Frank Miles. Born in Jersey in 1853, Emilie Charlotte le Breton was the only daughter of the Very Reverend William Corbet le Breton. At the age of 21 she married Edward Langtry, a shipowner, and they moved to London. Lillie was a great Victorian beauty, the famous portrait by Sir John Millais giving her the name 'The Jersey Lily'. Daisy, Countess of Warwick, wrote of her: 'she had dewy violet eyes, a complexion like a peach, how can words convey the vitality, the glow, the amazing charm that made this fascinating woman the centre of any group she entered'.

124.   A charming view of Langtry Manor, Derby Road, built by the Prince of Wales, later King Edward VII, for the beautiful Lillie Langtry. The residence was first called the Red House and the Prince often stayed nearby whilst it was being built. There is a foundation stone with 'E.L.L. 1877' engraved upon it. A stained glass window bears the date 1881, the year of the birth of Jeanne-Marie, Lillie's daughter. Lillie's and Edward's initials with intertwined hearts and the date 1883 are scratched into the pane of a downstairs window. On a wall near Lillie's suite are the words *Dulce Domum* – 'Sweet Home'.

125. This is known as the Edward VII room and remains today much as it must have looked over 100 years ago. This picture shows the original oak-beamed ceiling and the carved wooden fireplace with its blue and goldleaf tiles portraying Shakespearian scenes chosen by Lillie. On the wall outside are the words inscribed in stone *Stet Fortuna Domus*, 'May fortune attend those who dwell here'.

126. The dining room at Langtry Manor. Over the fireplace hangs a fine oil painting of Edward VII with his favourite hunting dog by Heywood Hardy. There is a delightful minstrel gallery, and high up in a corner of the room a tiny window, through which the Prince could inspect the guests before coming down to dine. The room is still the scene of lavish Victorian dinners arranged for the guests by the owner of this unusual hotel.

127. The Zig-Zag Path, a gradual descent from the top of the East Cliff, was a very pleasant and easy route down to the sands below. In the winter of 1908-9 the Council spent the sum of £300 making the Zig-Zag from Steps Chine, also known as Meyrick Steps.

128. The East Cliff lift. Note the delightful costumes and the ever present parasols. The platform at the top afforded spectacular views across the bay.

129.   Boscombe Chine early in this century. As Bournemouth grew, houses were built beyond the town since there was a great demand for accommodation. This area was once separated from Bournemouth by wild heathland. The Chine is a narrow valley running to the sea. All along this coast there are a number of villages with 'combe' as part of their names. During the 18th century the name was written as 'Boscomb', the final 'e' being added in the 19th century.

130.   An animated scene in Boscombe Crescent Gardens. An early resident was Sir Henry Drummond Wolff, the Member of Parliament for Christchurch. He purchased the estate of Boscombe Chine and Shore Lane as it was then known. He built for himself the house 'Boscombe Tower', the remainder of the land being used for villas.

"Boscombe Then and Now."

Boscombe in 1876.

Boscombe now.

131. This card was sent in 1905. It shows the roadway as it appeared in 1876, with the lower view the busy Boscombe scene a few decades later. It is difficult to imagine that this part was once isolated from Bournemouth, with just one or two cottages attached to smallholdings. There was also an inn, the *Palmerston Arms*, previously known as *The Ragged Cat*, thought to have been built as a halfway house between Pokesdown and Bournemouth.

132.   Linden Hall, Boscombe, will be recalled by many residents and visitors. This fine old building was demolished in 1986.

133.   A pretty scene showing the Rustic Bridge in Boscombe Gardens, a quiet and rural corner. The uniformed nurse with the basketwork baby carriage and the small girl in her white pinafore make a charming picture.

134.   Undercliff Terrace, Boscombe.

135.   The pond in the gardens, Boscombe. The sailing of miniature boats was a favourite pastime for children of all ages.

136. Undercliff Road, Boscombe, in Edwardian days. The ladies' costumes are of particular interest, as is the thatched shelter. In the centre of the road is an early mechanised omnibus, open-sided and canopied; the fare was one penny.

137. Boscombe pier was built by private enterprise in 1888. It was designed by Archibald Smith and constructed by E. Howell of the Waterloo Foundry Works, Poole. Lady Shelley drove in the first pile on 17 October 1888 and the pier was officially opened on 29 July 1889 by the Duke of Argyll. The pier was never very popular and proved unprofitable for its owners. At the turn of the century the skeleton of the 'Boscombe Whale' was exhibited on the pier. This was a 65-foot specimen of the North Atlantic whale which became stranded on the beach on 7 January 1897. A specially-made framework was created on the pier, and the whale proved a great attraction to visitors for a few years.

138.   Boscombe pier in its heyday when it was hoped that it would rival Bournemouth pier in popularity. It was purchased by Bournemouth Corporation and there was a grand re-opening in 1904. The provision of facilities for roller skating drew many younger people, but it never became really profitable.

139.   A view of Boscombe from the flagstaff. The area became well known because of its links with Sir Percy Florence Shelley, son of the poet, Percy Bysshe Shelley. He was born in Florence and gave his name to Florence Road. His mother is commemorated by Wollstonecraft Road, since she was the daughter of Mary Wollstonecraft Godwin. Mary Shelley was the author of *Frankenstein*.

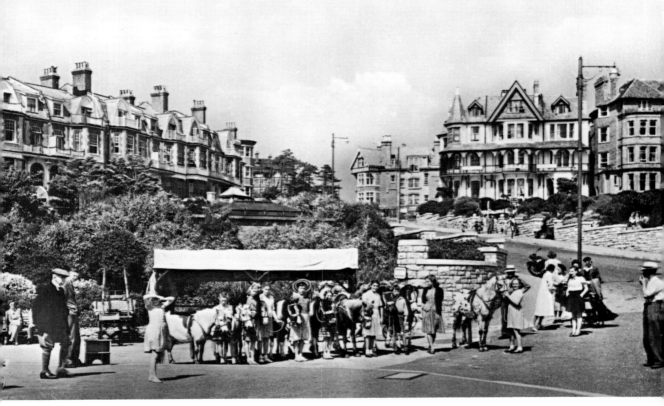

140.   Ponies on the promenade at Boscombe pier, a very popular attraction during the summer months.

141. The pier approach, Boscombe, *c.*1925.

142. Sea Road, formerly known as Shore Lane.

143. The golden sands of Boscombe in the early days of the century, with bathing machines at the water's edge. More and more villas were being built as the demand for accommodation grew. In the distance is Bournemouth pier with the Purbeck hills beyond.

144. The sands at Boscombe were ideal for family holidays and drew many visitors.

145. The Portman Ravine, Boscombe. The name Portman occurs frequently in the district because the second Mrs. Lewis Tregonwell was Henrietta Portman.

146. The road to Overcliff on the Portman Estate. This was next to the estate of Boscombe Manor, owned by Sir Percy Shelley. Lord Portman lived at Wentworth Lodge and the mansion remained in the family until 1922 when it became the Bournemouth Collegiate School for Girls.

147. Fisherman's Walk was the name originally given to a narrow path used by fishermen living nearby who walked down the cliffpath to their boats on the beach below. This was considered to be a good place to fish, for here the mackerel shoals came in. The men would then have a long haul back up the cliffs with their catch. Invariably they would make for the *New Bell Inn*, there being no other public house for many miles.

148. Seabourne Road, Pokesdown. Before the building of St Peter's church in Bournemouth, the only other place of worship was the Congregational chapel at Pokesdown, on the road between Poole and Christchurch, which was also used as a school.

149. The Cliff Steps, Pokesdown, with a surprisingly deserted beach. Some believe the curious name is derived from Puck's Down or Pixie's Down. At one time Pokesdown was just a small village on the road to Christchurch. It has a beautiful church, St James's, with a lovely interior. There has been much development in this area and the old village now merges into the borough of Bournemouth.

150. This is how much of the wild heathland between Christchurch and Bournemouth looked in Victorian days. Gradually the land was sold for building. Even today there are still stretches of moorland on the cliff edge at Boscombe, but now comfortable seats have been provided.

151.   Wimbourne Road, Winton. Trams arrived in this area in 1903. Several of the shopfronts will be recalled by older residents, including Bailey's, the men's hairdresser. In 1891 Winton had more than 4,000 inhabitants, and was a place in its own right, being separated from Bournemouth by rough undeveloped land. By 1899 the population had risen to 7,245. It became an Urban District in 1898, and part of Bournemouth in 1901.

152.   All Saints' church, West Southbourne. The pines are a striking feature of the site. Incorporated into Bournemouth in 1901, Southbourne was once a lonely place within the parish of Pokesdown. In 1870 a Bournemouth physician, Dr. T. A. Compton, bought 230 acres of land here for £3,000. He called it Southbourne-on-Sea, and visualised it as a future health resort.

153.   A rugged scene of the cliffs and seashore at West Southbourne. Dr. Compton's new resort had a pier and esplanade. In 1898 two French ships foundered on this exposed coast in heavy seas. The barque *Bonne Mère* from Le Havre was in difficulties on the morning of 24 November. She was taken in tow; but the *Marie Thérèse*, a three-masted brigantine, ran aground on the Beer Pan Rocks and was completely wrecked. The pier later became derelict and the whole area is now under the sea.

154.   Southbourne pier was opened on 2 August 1888. Designed by Archibald Smith, it was built by the Poole contractor Howell at a cost of £4,000. The opening was a great occasion with a visit by the steamer *Lord Elgin* from Bournemouth – daily excursions were made between the two piers. Sadly, within 20 years the pier, sea wall and esplanade had been severely damaged by storms and lay in ruins.

155.   The pleasant tree-lined Grand Avenue, Southbourne, shows how the land was developed from its wild state into a residential district. Dr. Compton had hoped it would rival Bournemouth as a health resort.

156.   A charming summer scene at Wick Ferry. The poled punt ferried visitors across the river Stour. The ferry was also used by wildfowlers who would mount a large gun on the front of the punt to shoot ducks. The river had been used by smugglers during the 18th and 19th centuries.

157. The large plantation known as Talbot Woods. In 1890 the number of pine trees in the area was thought to be 3,000,000 so it is not surprising that in that year Bournemouth took a pine tree for its crest. This is now a high class residential area.

158. Another look at the pier entrance, so very different from the view today. This leisurely scene recalls vividly a bygone age.

159.   A prime view of the famous Plummer's store, *c.*1920. It was situated near Gervis Place. The upper part of the building is now offices with shops at street level.

160.   The Pavilion and pier entrance before the fly-over was built. The New Baths were opened in 1936 and demolished in 1986.

161. A rare photograph of England's most famous cricketer, the great W. G. Grace, a legend even in his lifetime, seen here at Dean Park. William Gilbert Grace was born in 1848 at Downend, near Bristol, the fourth son of the village doctor. By the age of 18 he was already a distinguished cricketer. He played in many great matches at home, and made cricketing tours in Canada, the U.S.A. and Australia. He studied medicine at St Bartholomew's Hospital 1875-78, and took L.R.C.P. at Edinburgh in 1879. He settled in general practice in Bristol but still found time for many brilliant exhibitions of his favourite game. By 1895 he had scored a century 100 times.

162.   The name of R. H. Moore will be remembered by many cricket enthusiasts. He was a Bournemouth man, educated at Bournemouth School. In 1937 he made the highest individual score for Hampshire, 316. N. T. McCorkell was Hampshire's wicket-keeper. He played for the county between 1932 and 1951. He played in 383 matches, made 512 catches and 15,834 runs – an amazing record. As a wicket-keeper he dismissed more batsmen than any other Hampshire player.

BOURNEMOUTH CRICKET WEEK. TUES AUG 25

163. A photograph taken during Bournemouth Cricket Week at Dean Park, bearing the date 25 August 1914, probably the last county cricket match played here until after the First World War. The match was Hampshire against Lancashire. In this match Alec Bowell scored 204 in the first innings for Hampshire, out of a total of 377. The match ended in a draw. Alec Bowell played for Hampshire from 1902 until 1927 in 473 matches. This 204 was his best score ever. Cricket was first played at Dean Park in 1871. Hampshire county first class cricket has been played here since 1898.

NO 25.

THE "CHERRIES" FIRST TEAM, 1899-1900.

Back Row — KEATS.   J. SPICER.   J. C. NUTT, *President.*   S. DAVIS.   E. FRANCIS.   S. DRAPER, *Secretary.*
Sitting—C. SMITH, C. STEPHENSON, A. EMERY, *Captain,* C. KERLEY, J. HOOKEY, E. RICHARDSON.
Front — C. COXEN,   T. KERLEY.   H. HANHAM.

St. John's Institute, then B.F.C.

164.   This old photograph shows the 'Cherries' First Team. Prior to this there were several football clubs in the Bournemouth area from the early 1880s. This League Division III Club came into being in 1899. In their first season they competed in the Bournemouth and District Junior League for the Hampshire Junior Cup. For two seasons they played on a ground at Castlemain Road, Pokesdown, and paid £5 10s. for the season.

165. Mr. Wilfred Hayward, whose great hobby was the Boscombe Football Club. He became Secretary at the commencement of the 1905-6 season. The club prospered under his guidance and his flair for selecting promising players was well known. Mr. Hayward was the pioneer of professional football in Bournemouth. It was due to his enterprise that the club acquired its own home, the waste ground owned by Mr. J. E. Cooper Dean, now known as Dean Court.

166. From the commencement of the 1905-6 season rapid progress was made, the club graduating into senior amateur football in Hampshire and Dorset, winning most of the league and cup competitions which it entered. The Dean Court site had to be levelled and turfed, which was accomplished with the help of supporters. A stand was built to seat 300, and the ground was enclosed by a fence. This photograph shows the first team to play at Dean Court, in the 1910-11 season.

THE FIRST TEAM TO PLAY AT DEAN COURT, SEASON 1910-11.

Top Row—S. Knight, S. Blachford, W. Horne, A. Williams, P. Giles, P. Bennett, W. Clarkson, G. Parsley, W. Cassidy, H. Jenkins, J. Brown, W. Marsh, C. Richardson *(Hon. Sec.)*. *Middle Row*—H. T. Franklin *(President)*, C. Marsh, G. Smith, B. Penton, W. Hayward *(Hon. Sec.)* W. Tarrant, R. Whiterow, E. Manns. G. Hutchings. *Bottom Row*—C. Franklin, J. P. New, J. Small, P. Taylor, F. J. Franklin. HANTS LEAGUE CUP, WEST DIVISION.

167. Bournemouth's first professional league team, for the season 1923-24. The change of title to Bournemouth and Boscombe Athletic Football Club made it more representative of the whole borough. The first season was uphill work, but during the 1924-25 season the team acquired some first class players including Ron Eyre from Sheffield Wednesday, and Leslie Roberts and Pat Clifford from Merthyr Town.

168.   There was great excitement for the opening of the new stand at Dean Court by Mr. C. E. Sutcliffe, Vice-President of the Football League, on the first day of the season, 27 August 1927. The steel framework of the stand was purchased from Wembley, after the British Empire Exhibition closed. The cost was almost £12,000. This ambitious scheme was made possible through the generosity of the ground landlord, who had granted a long lease at a nominal rent. The stand was erected in four months during the closed season, a great achievement.

169.   An exciting incident in the 'Wolves' goalmouth during the F.A. Cup-Tie (third round) at Dean Court during the 1947-48 season. The picture shows Bert Williams, the Wolves goalkeeper, making a spectacular save from a Bournemouth attack. The Bournemouth player is Freddie Rowell, here pictured next to Billy Wright, the Wolverhampton Wanderers captain.

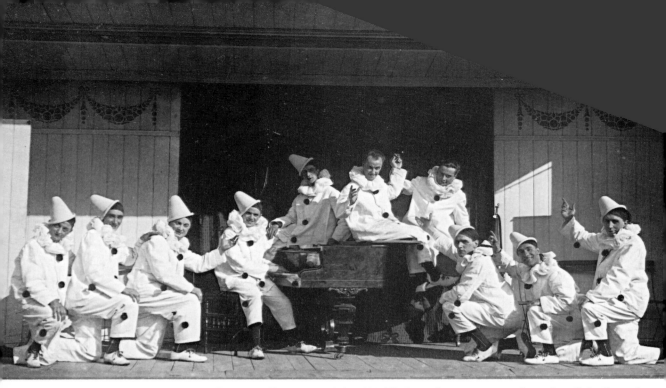

170. The Birchmore and Lindon Pierrots at Bournemouth in 1915. Various pierrot troops performed until the Second World War. This group performed to the east of the pier and the Gay Cadets performed about 300 yards to the west.

171. The B.B.C. Wireless Studio in Holdenhurst Road during the 1920s or 1930s. This was Bournemouth's first local radio and Bertram Fryer is at the microphone. The room looks simple and uncluttered by comparison with the vast array of technical equipment in modern studios.

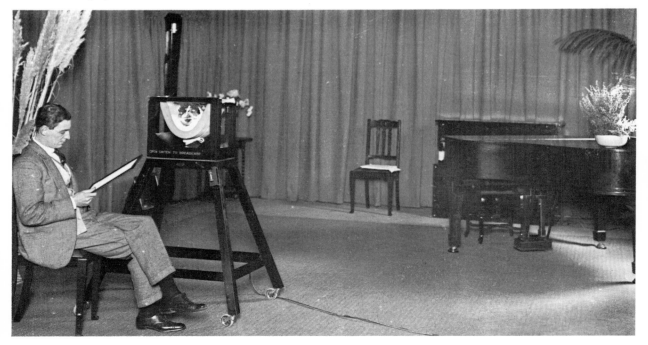

VIOLET VANBRUGH

172.   The beautiful and famous Miss Violet Vanbrugh. One of London's most talented actresses in her day, she came down to Bournemouth many times to act on the stage of the Theatre Royal. She sent this photograph to the author, and on the reverse has written 'I wish you every good and happy wish for your first term at the R.A.D.A.'.

MR. DAN GODFREY.

BOURNEMOUT

173. The original Bournemouth Municipal Orchestra at the Winter Gardens. This orchestra achieved world fame under the direction of Dan Godfrey. He was in his mid-twenties when he came to Bournemouth in 1893 as conductor; within the year he became Musical Director. He was knighted in 1922 for his services to municipal music.

174.   A relaxed and happy scene at the Overstrand Café, Boscombe.